PRISONERS OF
TRANSIENCE

Also by Sheenagh Pugh:
Earth Studies and other voyages (1982)

PRISONERS OF TRANSIENCE

Sheenagh Pugh

POETRY WALES PRESS
1985

POETRY WALES PRESS, 56 PARCAU AVENUE, BRIDGEND,
MID GLAMORGAN

© Sheenagh Pugh, 1985

British Library Cataloguing in Publication Data

Prisoners of transience.
1. Poetry, Modern − Translations into English
2. English poetry − Translations from foreign
literature
I. Pugh, Sheenagh
808.81'032   PN6100

ISBN 0-907476-46-5

Cover Design: Cloud Nine Design
Cover Illustration: 'Soldat' by Conrad Meyer

Published with the financial support of the
Welsh Arts Council

TYPESET BY AFAL, CARDIFF
PRINTED IN CHELTENHAM BOOK
by
Antony Rowe Ltd.,
Chippenham

Contents

"It is the proof of intelligence, the proof of not being a barbarian, to be able to enter into something outside of oneself, something that does not touch one's next neighbour in the city omnibus."

Robert Louis Stevenson: Vailima Letters, 1894

Introduction

It is possible to go on for a long time about the purposes and methods of translation. I shall try not to. My *reason* for translating these particular poets is that I liked them and wished to share them with others. My *purposes* in each case were: to render as faithfully as I could the actual words of the poet and the sense of what he/she wished to convey: to reproduce as far as I could something of his/her own sound; the individual voice if you like: and to do all this in decent English. I have frequently found myself having to adjust the relative claims of these priorities; I have tried never to totally abandon one in favour of another.

The kind of poem I am translating tended to be written in strict forms − rondeaux, ballades, sonnets − and, with the proviso that half-rhyme both comes more naturally to me and sounds more natural in modern English verse than full rhyme, I have reproduced them. There are of course different opinions as to whether a translator should reproduce the forms of the original. I do it because I do not believe a poet chooses a particular form for nothing; he must have felt this form somehow assisted what he meant to say and, since the meaning of poetry is carried on the level of sound as well as that of sense, I risk being false to him if I ignore how he chose to sound. The obvious alternative argument is that one can achieve a more literal translation by ignoring formal considerations. I would say only that one can of course achieve the highest possible standard of accuracy − on one level − in a straight prose translation, but I think not many poets would actually choose to be translated that way.

Two specific 'formal' problems arose. Firstly, it may be argued that as English isn't a particularly rhyming language it would make sense to cheat on the French ballades, with their murderous rhyme-scheme, by abandoning the continuity of rhyme from verse to verse. There is an illustrious precedent for this, namely Charles d'Orléans, who translated some of his ballades into English that way. He had, however, the excuse that he was working in a language foreign to him, and there are arguments on the other side. For me, at least, the ballades do lose a certain resonance and inevitability if one does this. It is also possible to overestimate the difficulties. Certainly if one were looking only for good, strong, pure rhymes, one would look a long time and fatally injure the sense of the verse. But the French rhymes are nothing of the sort; they are in fact generally very weak, relying heavily on certain common terminations and verb-forms – the standard -er -esse -ais, etc. It is the sort of rhyme intended to create an unobtrusive background resonance and its English equivalent strikes me as being half-rhyme or thereabouts.

Secondly, German sonnets of the 17th century were almost always written in alexandrines, because their writers were very influenced by French models. Alexandrines can sound a bit on the ponderous side in German, but nothing like as bad as they do in English. I have translated into iambic pentameter because that has always been the natural metre for sonnets in English, as the alexandrine was in its day in German. It may be noted that when the bilingual Weckherlin wrote a sonnet in English, he used the iambic pentameter.

I suppose, just possibly, someone might raise the question of not *how*, but *if* one should translate poets from the 12th, 14th, 17th centuries – are these persons still 'relevant' to us and our concerns. I would refer them to two quotations; that from Robert Louis Stevenson which prefaces this book, and this from William Cavendish, tutor of the young Charles II, and thus contemporary of many of the 17th-century poets here: "What you would read I would have it history, that so you might compare the dead with the living, for the same humours is now as was then; there is no alteration but in names".

From the French

Christine de Pisan 1363?-1429?

Daughter of an Italian doctor, she was married at about 16 to a secretary at the French court. About 10 years later, he died, leaving her with three children, a lot of creditors and not much money. Since she did not care to remarry, she needed a profession and she took up writing for money. Her first theme was the grief of her widowhood, on which she was eloquent, but this didn't sell well to a public that emphatically did not want anything autobiographical or confessional from its poets. What it wanted was the celebration, within prescribed conventions, of courtly love. Christine, on the principle that the customer is always right, cheerfully complied. Later, when the children were off her hands and she had less need of money, she wrote what she really liked, which was political, reflective and satirical verse. In about 1418 she retired, as gentlewomen often did, to a convent, and is not known to have written again except for one poem in 1429, in praise of Joan of Arc, who had just raised the siege of Orleans.

She was at pains to stress that none of her courtly love poems was autobiographical. This did not prevent them from being original; her imaginary ladies are allowed to share much of her humour and good sense, and of course her viewpoint on the game is, per se, an unusual one — it is common for the lover to complain that he is in floods of tears owing his lady's reticence, but one doesn't often, as in *'Mon ami, ne plourez plus,'* hear the woman's response — kind, amused and more than slightly deflating. Neither were the conventional forms purely restrictive: the circular movement of the rondeau, for instance, is well suited to expressing a mood, as may be seen in *'Source de plour, riviere de tristesse'* and in *'Il a au jour d'uy un mois'* she uses the insistent rondeau refrain with stunning effect to stress the central fact reverberating in the woman's mind. Technically she has some very individual characteristics such as her freedom in placing the caesura and her preference for run-on lines, producing a natural, conversational movement — she has a distinctly chatty style, which I have tried, probably in vain, to reproduce.

Source de plour, riviere de tristesse

Spring of tears, river of misery,
ocean of bitterness, flood-tide of pain
surrounds me, drowns my sad heart that can
suffer too well; feel too acutely.

I'm sunk now; plunged deep in agony,
it sweeps over me, stronger than Seine,
spring of tears, river of misery,

and the great waves all surge above me
as if the wind of fate drove them in.
I hardly think that I shall rise again,
so beaten down I am, and they so high,
spring of tears, river of misery.

Vostre doulçour mon cuer attrait

Your gentleness draws me to you:
I'm done with hesitancy.
Why, when love speaks to me
from your eyes, would I say no?

Indeed I love, and shall not go
back on love, for honestly
your gentleness draws me to you.

Now be all mine, and all true,
and our days that are to be
shall pass in ease and pleasantry.
In your fair face, shining through,
your gentleness draws me to you.

Mon ami, ne plourez plus!

My friend, please don't cry!
I can't stand it; you're so good
at moving sympathy, that I
will freely give all you could
desire in love. It's time to mend
your looks; cheer up for me, now.
For heaven's sake, make an end!
Whatever you want, I want too.

Nor need you worry, nor lie
in hiding, under a cloud,
but learn now to be happy,
for love ought not to be proud
towards merit, and I intend
to grant all your wishes, since you
have done so well. You may depend,
whatever you want, I want too.

Indeed I'm limed, persuaded by
love, and still more, that great flood
of tears: I've no wish to die
by drowning, dear; who would?
I'm there for you; I won't pretend,
come on then, hold me; do!
I am your most dear friend:
whatever you want, I want too.

Cil qui m'a mis en pensée nouvelle

The man on whom my mind has lately run,
who asks my love, pleases me very well,
though you need not suppose that I shall tell
him so; that's not how things ought to be done.

And yet he is a pleasant gentleman,
young, beautiful, more tender than a girl,
the man on whom my mind has lately run.

I must care for my reputation,
so I dare neither call him mine, nor feel
as I could do, though someone so genteel
deserves my love, or that of anyone,
the man on whom my mind has lately run.

Tu soies le tres bien venu

'I'm very glad to see you,
my dear! Give me a kiss.
And how did everything go
on your travels? Have you always
been well and happy? Come, then,
sit down by me and relate
the whole story: how've you been?
I want a full account of that.'

'My lady, whom I'm bound to
above all others, know this:
without you, desire nagged so
that I never rejoiced less.
Love placed my heart under a ban,
commanding me: "Keep faith now, at
all costs, for when you come again
I want a full account of that."'

'Why then, you have been true
to your word, and good it is
to hear! And since you're home now
in health, we may be at our ease.
But now tell me, if you can,
by how much agony your state
has been worse than my pain.
I want a full account of that.'

'Oh, mine was worse, I maintain,
but first tell me, at what rate
of kisses will you pay your man?
I want a full account of that.'

Il a au jour d'uy un mois

It was just a month ago
that my friend went away.

I'm still feeling very low:
it was just a month ago.

'Goodbye', he said, 'I'm off now',
and that was all he would say,
It was just a month ago.

Les roys, les princes et les sages

Princes, kings and men of lore,
the men of days that are long gone,
used often to set great store
by things now out of fashion.
They valued reputation:
getting rich didn't rate so high.
But now, he who can keep his own
has learned enough to get by.

What's a great man renowned for?
Prowess, honour, dominion;
that he was generous, or knew more
than most; so his deeds live on.
But now the most honour is shown
to him who keeps his charity
firmly in check; such a man
has learned enough to get by.

These grasping gentry make the poor
suffer great wrong and affliction.
'Yours' is a word they deplore,
but 'mine', oh, that's well known.
Now he who gets his hands upon
more money, by chicanery,
or graft, or however he can,
has learned enough to get by.

Il vous est pris bien en sursault

It seemed to come on very soon,
this love that so afflicts you,
and you soon make your wishes known,
sir; no-one could call you slow.
This just isn't how to do
things: where would my wits be
if I loved you so readily?

I've always heard that a man
who wants love should earn it through
endurance and affliction.
You ask too much: I'll have you know
I'm no such miss; besides, it's true
that you'd be first to blame me
if I loved you so readily.

And I think a woman has done
ill by her honour, and yours too,
if she rates cheap what everyone
who loves at all should value
beyond price. Your repute would go
no higher, sir, for having me,
if I loved you so readily.

Charles d'Orléans 1394-1465

Things tended to happen to him. His childhood was happy and privileged enough, as the son of the Duke of Orleans. With youth, the rot set in; both his parents died – his father murdered by political enemies – and an adolescent marriage to his cousin Isabelle (widow of Richard II as it happens), ended in her early death. She is the subject of the poem *'J'ay fait l'obsèque de ma Dame,'* here translated. Meanwhile Charles was heavily involved with the blood-feud for his father – he wore black for some years, until he could arrange a revenge killing. He then left off mourning, remarried and presumably felt, at the age of 21, that it might be time to relax a bit. Unfortunately the battle of Agincourt intervened. Having spent most of the battle concussed under a heap of dead, he was taken as a prisoner of war to England, where he remained for the next 25 years, being used as a political bargaining counter. As a duke, his imprisonment was not particularly harsh, but many poems testify to his frustration at seeing great events go on without him in his homeland (including Joan of Arc's campaign to raise the siege of his native Orleans). When he got back, his second wife and a considerable number of his acquaintance were dead. He was, however, despite his haunted, pessimistic side, a resilient man; he married again, started a family and spent his time writing, socialising and, one hopes, finally doing more or less as he liked.

The habit of personifying one's thoughts and emotions is not unique to him, but in his long imprisonment he took it further than anyone, peopling what must often have been a lonely world with such abstractions as Tristesse, Melancolie and Nonchaloir (roughly translatable as a feeling of sod-it-all). His verse is the verbal equivalent to the pictures in a mediaeval Book of Hours; formal yet alive with a wealth of detail, coloured like jewels.

J'ay fait l'obsèque de ma Dame

My wife's body lies in state
in love's chapel, and I call
my pain-racked thought to celebrate
the mass for her immortal soul.
The candles of her burial
flame softly, like the breath of sighs.
Her coffin's made of memories
painted with tears; you may perceive
how all around, rich letters run,
saying: Here lies, without question,
the best of all this world can give.

She has a cloth of gold, set
with blue sapphires, for a pall,
since gold stands for fortunate
and sapphire means immutable.
They suit well her funeral,
for it was those same qualities
God meant to set before our eyes
when His hands went to contrive
a thing of such perfection.
I speak plain: she stood alone,
the best of all this world can give.

I can't talk about that
any more; my heart is full
when I hear any relate
her virtues; she had them all,
as those will swear, both great and small,
who knew her. Now God's pleasure is
to grace his park of Paradise
with her person; so I believe,
for that is where she should be gone
who seemed to every kind of man
the best of all this world can give.

23

As useless to complain as grieve;
we all shall die, late or soon.
It won't stay long with anyone,
the best of all this world can give.

En regardant vers le pays de France

At Dover by the sea as once I was,
I happened somehow to be looking out
to France, and all my former happiness,
upon a sudden, rose into my throat
from deep inside. My breath came hard; I fought
for air, and yet it still comforted me
to see France where my heart is bound to be.

I told myself it was a foolish case
to let my heart get into such a rut,
when I could see things moving towards peace
and all the blessings that it brings about.
With such wisdom I comforted my thought;
it didn't stop me looking constantly
to see France where my heart is bound to be.

There is a ship named Hope; it sails apace,
freighted with all my longings, and it's got
sealed orders to commend me to that place
over the sea, the home where I am not
and can't come, without peace: God send us that!
A speedy peace, and my delivery
to see France where my heart is bound to be.

A treasure beyond all that can be bought
is peace; we cannot praise it as we ought.
I hate this war that will not set me free
to see France where my heart is bound to be.

En la forest d'Ennuyeuse Tristesse

In the dark wood of grief I chanced to meet
Venus herself, as I walked aimlessly
in loneliness, and when she saw my state,
she stopped at once, wishing to know of me
where I was going. 'Why, necessity,'
I said, 'long since determined to impound
me here: I might be called, objectively,
a wandering man who wonders where he's bound.'

'My dear,' she said, 'I am surprised at that.
How can I help you? I would willingly,
for truth to tell, I thought I saw you set
long ago on a path I had made free
of thorns, the way of pleasure. Who is he,
I wonder, who has turned you so around?
Now it distresses me indeed to see
a wandering man who wonders where he's bound.'

'Lady, I see no need of this debate;
I think you surely know my history.
That Death who deals such mischief took my mate,
the one I loved so much, my company,
my only hope. So good a guide was she
that in her lifetime I was never found
as I am now, needing your sympathy,
a wandering man who wonders where he's bound.

Now it's gone dark: I feel my destiny
as blind men do their path, so carefully
tap-tapping with a stick along the ground.
My grief it is that I was born to be
a wandering man who wonders where he's bound.'

En tirant d'Orléans à Blois

Going to Blois the other day
by water, as I've often done,
I saw vessels scudding away
in a fine, easy fashion
before the wind, and each one
sailed a straight course up the river,
for they had, as was well shown,
a fair wind in their favour.

I was watching this display
with all my thought and emotion,
and I whispered: that's the way
I wish I were; I'd surely run
the sail of relaxation
up on my ship; only that never
in all my time have I known
a fair wind in my favour.

For good fortune stands at stay
as my life's ship sails upon
her course. I row, as best I may,
with hope for oars, but I am grown
weary in long affliction,
becalmed, for all my endeavour.
I'd wait long, if I counted on
a fair wind in my favour.

Upstream those ships were quickly gone,
while I pulled, on my way down,
against the waves of pain, as ever.
If He will, may God send soon
a fair wind in my favour.

Rondeau

(Addressed to one M. Nevers, who had been the guest of
Charles and his wife.)

You've been our guest: now you must pay.
Leave us your heart, sir, when you go.
You must come back, and you may know
we'll guard it well against that day.

Content yourself; no other way
can please us; only this will do.
You've been our guest: now you must pay.

But, dearest sir, if you should say
we ask too much, we'll manage so:
I'll willingly change hearts with you,
and mine shall go, and yours shall stay.
You've been our guest: now you must pay.

Le temps a laissié son manteau

The world has left her winter wear
of rain and cold and windy sky,
and has put on embroidery
of glancing sunlight, blond and clear.

No beast, no bird of the air
but in its tongue can sing or cry:
'The world has left her winter wear.'

Rivers, streams, waters everywhere
go in a glittering livery
of jewelled silver. Now we'll be
new dressed; cast off the coat of care.
The world has left her winter wear.

From the German

Walther von der Vogelweide 1170?-1230?

Birthplace unknown. He was attached to the court at Vienna in his youth, but became persona non grata there around 1198, possibly due to his feud with the court poet Reinmar von Hagenau, and took to the road. For most of his subsequent life he had no fixed residence and attached himself to various political patrons for a living. There were plenty of these handy, as two families were at the time quarrelling for the title of German Emperor. Walther's dependence on these individuals led to his becoming a political propagandist, ready to aid his patrons with powerful verse in return for protection, or to turn the full blast of his satire on them if he thought he wasn't getting paid enough. He was a prickly, cantankerous man, and he had very little personal loyalty to anyone – loyalty was something he rented out temporarily in exchange for money. All this was at least partly due to his lifelong financial insecurity and since he held Reinmar, his Vienna rival, responsible for some of this, his lament for Reinmar shows some magnanimity – plus a lot of honesty. Walther was in a dilemma; as Reinmar's fellow-poet and ex-colleague he was bound as a matter of courtesy to write an elegy, but since it was well known that he had hated the man, he had to avoid being accused of hypocrisy. Hence a rather unorthodox poem. Both for his political verse and his love-poems (which with their realism and honesty finally killed off courtly love verse in Germany), Walther is considered the greatest German poet of his time.

Walther's Lament for Reinmar

I mourn you, Reinmar, honestly,
 – a damn sight more than you would me,
if you were living, and it was I lay dead. –
Let's be frank now, and speak it out:
you, as a man, I could live without.
I grieve for your great art, with you decayed.
Oh, you could lift the heart of any man,
when you wrote as you knew it should be done.
I mourn your mouth of a true poet: I mourn your gentle
song.

I mourn that I in my time saw their end.
You might have waited just a while, my friend,
I could have borne you company; I shan't be singing long.
Good journey to your soul, and all my thanks, Reinmar,
to your tongue.

Heinrich von Morungen birthdate unknown, died 1220

Little is known of his life except that he probably came from Thüringen, was in the service of one Dietrich von Meissen, and is traditionally supposed to have visited the Orient. (This is possible; Meissen went on the 1197 crusade and Morungen could have accompanied him.) He writes of courtly love, like all his contemporaries, but very differently from most of them. Most courtly love-poems, at least until Walther von der Vogelweide, take place in the mind; it is a poetry of ideas, feelings, abstracts. Morungen's poems are sharply visualised, full of practical details, sudden flashes of light and colour. Possibly because of this, they are also rather more erotic than most. (The situation in 'Tagelied' is of course the normal one in an aubade; the lady is married, and the knight who is her lover must make himself scarce at daybreak.) He is also noted for flashes of psychological insight; in *'Mirst geschên'* he comes very close, in the imagery he chooses, to admitting the central fact about courtly love-poetry, namely that the lady who is its object exists mainly in the man's mind.

Dawnsong
(Tagelied)

(Man) Oh God, will ever her body,
so well-made, more white
than a fall of snow, guide me
again; gleam in my night?
It deceived my eyes;
I took it for no less
than the moon's brightness:
then the day came.

(Lady) Oh God, will he ever
spend time here again,
when for us night is over,
that we need not complain
'hell, here comes the day'.
Always, when he lay
with me, that's what he'd say:
then the day came.

(Man) Oh God, she kissed me, still
asleep, times out of mind,
and her tears fell and fell,
and there was no end,
and I tried to ease
her, and the cries
stopped, and she held me close:
then the day came.

(Lady) Oh God, why has he feasted
his eyes so on me!
When he drew from my bed
the quilt, he liked to see
my poor body bare.
It never bored him, never:
that was a real wonder.
Then the day came.

Mirst geschên als eime kindelîne

It is with me as with a little child
who sees a fair reflection in the glass,
and, grasping for a face that can't be held,
shivers it into fragments; happiness
turned suddenly to anguish and disease.
And I thought my joy would have no end,
when I first saw that woman, my sweet friend,
the source of joy wherein my sorrow was.

Love who puts all the world in pleasure's way,
you brought that woman in a dream to me,
and made me, as in sleep my body lay,
to see with my own eyes, most hungrily,
my body's greatest joy... And the lovely
white gleam on her; perfect, but, to say
truly, that a slight tremor seemed to play
about her red mouth rich in ecstasy.

A great fear grasped me, thinking it might pale
at last, that mouth, and it so small and red,
and now I have this new cause of ill
to weigh on me. For sorrow am I made,
since my eyes opened on the thing I need,
like the child who, so unknowing still,
sees his own beauty's shadow in the well,
and loves all the way down until he's dead.

The wide band of heaven does not contain
a woman of a higher heart or mind
than her whose company I must refrain
for fear of harm, yet leave my heart behind.
I thought a love of such high wondrous kind
must have an end; I see I'm in
no more than the beginning of my pain,
and it's my soul's peace that is at an end.

Hartmann von Aue 1150?-1210?

Born somewhere in South Germany, a knight in the service of a feudal lord, he wrote lyric poems and verse epics. In his lyric verse he is distinguished by his humour and refusal to take seriously the cult of courtly love with its self-induced suffering, stating bluntly his preference for the village girls from whom he could obtain something rather more concrete than elevated thoughts. His verse epics include two Arthurian tales, a legend of a saint, and the enchanting story of *Der arme Heinrich,* a lord who is stricken with leprosy but cured by the joint intervention of God and a very determined peasant girl, whom the lord marries.

The description of this lord in the early part of the poem – young, rich, handsome, endowed with all the virtues, 'a flower of youth, a mirror of the world's joy', has been supposed to allude to the young lord of Aue, in whose service Hartmann was. The sudden death of this man, and, still more, the thought of his soul in purgatory, seems to have devastated Hartmann. At all events, he did something fairly dramatic about it. The Church at the time promised knights who went on crusade automatic entry into heaven, without the pains of purgatory. Hartmann went on a crusade, but dedicated it to his dead lord, so that the latter's soul would be the one released from pain. His two crusade-songs are here translated.

Kreuzlied 1

It is the cross makes a man scour
                            both act and heart,
that he in blessedness and honour
                            may have his part.
It is a strong security
                 to him whose flesh
contends with him for mastery;
                       it does not wish

to see him act as if
he alone owned his life,
nor wear the crusade's sign
on his breast, and emptiness within.

Now all our chivalry must give
                         their brave young days
to serve His turn through whom they live
                       in wealth and ease.
That knight who gave the world the use
                      of arm and sword
would be a damned fool to refuse
                  this greatest lord.

If he goes as God's man,
he surely shall attain
the two things he most craved —
the world's praise, and his soul saved.

The world gave me a swindler's grin
                       and set her lure,
so I was duly taken in
                and followed her.

The thorns of pleasure hedged me round
                                        such a long time;
where folly was, I would be found,
                            right in the swim.

Now help me, Christ my King,
whose journey I am going,
to count all this no loss
that I forsook, to take your cross.

Ever since death was pleased to thieve
                                    my lord from me,
whatever else the world can give
                            I can let be.
Most of life's pleasure goes with love,
                            the day it dies.
I may as well start thinking of
                        my soul and his.

This journey I undertake
for him and his soul's sake,
that we may meet at last
before God. I'll see him there: I must.

Kreuzlied 2

I go with your good grace, my friends and kin.
Good luck my land: good luck my people too.
None need ask why I made this journey mine.
I have affirmed all that I mean to do.
Love took me; set me free on my parole
and now commands me by my love to go.
I can no other; I surely must do so,
if I'm to keep my word and honour whole.

Many men boast what they would do for love.
Where are the deeds? Their words are prodigal,
but I never heard one ask to serve
the cause of love in the way that I shall.
That's love, that drives a man to take the course
of exile, as my words now drive me on;
for if my lord still lived, I'd not have gone
a step for Saladin and all his force.

You poets of love, you often sing in vain,
because your object is a fantasy.
No: when it comes to love-songs, I'm your man,
since I have love and love possesses me.
I love what loves me; where I wish to lie
is where I'm wanted; you were born to lose.
Poor lovers, seeking love that has no use
for you, how can you love such love as I?

Georg Rodolf Weckherlin 1584-1653

Born in Schwaben but lived many years in England, where he held office under Cromwell as Latin Secretary (bequeathing the job to one John Milton). He wrote also in Latin, French and English. Rondeaux are of course totally untypical of German verse of this or any period; he was amusing himself with a French verse-form that appealed to his sense of humour and liking for technical challenges.

Rondeau to Marina

(An die Marina: Rondeau)

Well you know what an agony
I have been in; what injury
your guiltless gentleness has done.
I have long burned under the brown
 light of your eyes; what more can I
say, since love so suddenly
has struck at both of us; only
that one thing now can help us: one.
Well you know what.

In brief, I wish you'd be as free
with kisses as you've been to me
with all the pain I've undergone.
Now, seeing we two are alone,
let's cast caution aside, and try
... well, you-know-what.

Poets of the Thirty Years' War

The Thirty Years' War (1618-1648) and its troubled
aftermath brought most ordinary German people an
embarrassing choice of ways to die. If by any chance the
war itself didn't get you, there was always infancy,
childbirth, disease, starvation or the general violence of the
times. In this situation a number of poets arose, chiefly in
Silesia but some too in the south, whose principal
characteristic was a keen awareness of the proximity of
death to life. Their daily observation taught them that life
was fragile and death imminent; that virtue, wisdom,
beauty, friendship were no more immune from violent
destruction than were folly and evil, and that nothing they
could see, except maybe the stars, had any permanence at
all. Everything that they saw became for them a mask, a
surface; behind it may be perceived transience and
mortality, beyond it, perhaps, the hope of something more
lasting and meaningful. Some sought comfort by belittling
this life and turning their minds on that eternity where they
hoped to find some permanence. Others, on the contrary
saw the impermanence of this life as a reason to enjoy it as
much as possible while they could, turning away in their
work from the fear of death which inspired them. The
greatest, like Gryphius, tackled the fragility of life head-on,
mourned for it and tried to see some purpose in it, both in
temporal and eternal terms.

Now that science has enabled us all to live in such close
proximity to death, it does seem to me that the situation and
preoccupations of these poets do not markedly differ from
our own. We may not be able to share their solutions to the
problem that haunted them (though we shall be lucky if we
can find any others), but we can surely share with some
painful interest their feelings about it.

Andreas Gryphius 1616-1664

His childhood reflects the disturbance of his times. He was born in Glogau, Silesia, child of the third marriage of a Lutheran archdeacon. His father died when Andreas was five; next year his mother, now looking after the children from all three of her late husband's marriages, herself remarried, to a teacher, Herr Eder. Six years later she too died, and Eder in turn remarried the following year. It will be noted that Andreas was now living with neither of his original parents, while his older half-brother Paul was now with his third stepmother. This lady proved popular with her stepchildren, so Andreas was further upset when she died in 1637. In this, Andreas' 21st year, he also saw the death of Paul's baby daughter Mariana in the fire of Freystadt, and wrote his famous epitaph for her. His first publication of German verse dates from this time (he had published some Latin verse as an adolescent). He studied at Leyden and became a public official, keenly interested in mathematics, astronomy and anatomy. He was by now in constantly bad health. The procession of death in his family continued; only one of his seven children survived him.

It is no wonder if, as anatomist and astronomer, he tended to look at the bones of life, and the stars beyond it. The war and the general proximity of death are central themes of his work as of his life; what is remarkable is the dispassionate, impersonal way he often manages to deal with them. He is a sober, powerful observer of his time, with a gift for creating certain emblematic images (like the storm-tossed ship of 'Vanitas Mundi') which recur throughout his work, gaining in power and intensity. He wrote both poems and plays, including one about his contemporary Charles I of England.

46

Epitaph of Mariana Gryphius, little daughter of the poet's brother Paul
(Grabschrift Marianae Gryphiae, seines Brudern Pauli Töchterlein)

I: born in flight, breathing the smoke of war,
ringed round with fire and steel, my father's care,
my mother's pain, was thrust into the light
as my land sank in angry burning night.
I saw the world, and soon I looked away,
since all its terrors met me on one day.
Though I died young, if but my days be told,
count up my fears, and I was very old.

(Mariana was a very young refugee. The night she was born, her home town of Freystadt burned down; the family fled and she died on the journey.)

Thoughts on time
(Betrachtung der Zeit)

Those years are not now mine, that have gone by.
No more are those that may come presently.
The moment's mine, and if I treasure this,
He's mine, who made both time and timelessness.

On the marriage of his niece Anna Maria to Herr Baum

(Auf H. Ditterich Baums und Jungfrau Annae Mariae Gryphiae Hochzeit)

You, madam bride, are fortunate indeed
that in this season, when the heat of war
and battle's flames all our sad harvest are,
the fires of love afford you sheltering shade.
Sit by your Tree and pay grim fate no heed,
who chars our land before we are aware,
who comes to scythe the meadows' fruitful fare,
the garden's blossom, with his burning blade.

This Tree you chose will always cover you;
you need fear nothing the dark storms can do,
the lovely leaves above you crowd the sky,
and see: these branches now so full of bloom
shall yield your longed-for fruit in time to come.
Believe me dear, this green can never die.

(The groom's name, Baum, means 'tree'. Hence the image of fruit, hence also the echo of this image in the next poem, wherein Gryphius learns that marriage and motherhood aren't quite the safe refuge he thought.)

On the death of his niece Anna Maria
(Annae Mariae Gryphiae Tod)

You dead ... you. Heaven would not have you stay
where vice is praised and virtue has no place,
where sins are all excused. We drove out grace,
and now she takes back you. Why did you say
goodnight so soon, when I was far away?
The lamps still burn that lit your first embrace,
but that's divorced, and I your death must face,
who was bereft even by your wedding-day.

I cannot reach you with my absent grief,
nor your frail fruit, whose opening so brief
closed its weak eyes and set your spirit free.
Just once, I wished I might see faith bear fruit,
who flourishes alone on virtue's root,
but fate would not permit my wish to be.

To the stars
(An die Sternen)

Oh lights who never sate my mortal eyes,
torches who split the cloudy dark of night,
oh diamond fires, your facets ever bright,
who bloom upon the wide fields of the skies.
You watchmen; when God dealt out destinies,
Wisdom His word first christened you aright,
who may be known and scanned but in God's sight
(we blinded mortals, how should we be wise?)

Oh pledges of my joy, to gaze on you
I leave my sleep and wake the sweet night through.
You heralds of that time, when will it be
that I, whose thoughts on earth rose all above,
whose spirit was infected with your love,
freed from all care, shall see you under me?

Vanitas Mundi

What may she be,
this world, whose beauty fooled me for so long?
How suddenly
death despoils poor and wealthy, old and young!
Why, what is all that here a man may find?
A passing wind.

What blooms today,
evening treads down. You see, a man may slave
his life away
for the brief gold he can't take to his grave.
He hoards for people he has never known
and dies alone.

That insect small
which spins a web, is tangled in its thread.
So do we all
most diligently labour to be dead,
and all our wit but leads us on the way
to quick decay.

The tulips glow,
and young girls cut them for their beauty down.
Girls fare just so,
for beauty brings disgrace on many a one,
with fear and pain, unless Death kindly come
to call them home.

If you stand high,
envy will raise your faults to mock your state;
if low you lie,
your fellow-men grind you beneath their feet.
The rich have only hate and bitterness:
the poor, still less.

As restlessly
as little boats from wind to wind are tossed,
so wander we
in storms of sorrow, and are all but lost
on this life's ocean, which is made of tears
and heavy cares.

What bliss he knows
who safely gains the harbour of the skies,
who wisely chose
that fleet's true course which sails for paradise.
Though waves like mountains tower on the sea,
storm-proof is he.

The misery of being human
(Menschliches Elende)

What's a man, then? The dwelling-house of pain,
a jack o' lantern, ball that chance has tossed,
a stage of fear, where suffering heads the cast,
a melting snowfall, a light on the wane.
Our life's like a brief chat, fleeting and vain,
and those who've left the flesh in which they dressed
and entered death's long casualty list
are from our thoughts, as if they had not been.

As lightly as a dream, yet with the force
of some great river, changeless in its course,
so do our name and praise pass out of mind.
What now breathes air must vanish with a breath,
what's not yet born will follow us to death,
and we shall be like smoke on a strong wind.

Evening

(Abend)

Swift day is run; star armies march behind
night's banner. Men in weary company
leave field and labour; where beasts used to lie,
loneliness grieves. Why, time's gone like the wind.
Those men are little boats, and soon they'll find
their port; light fails; so soon shall you and I,
and all we have, and all we see, pass by.
A racetrack life stretches before my mind.

Oh Lord, let me not slip upon the way,
nor pleasure, pain nor fear lead me astray.
Thy constant light lead me and live in me,
that, though my body sleep, my soul may wake,
and when my evening and the last day break,
then tear me from the darkness' vale to thee.

On the birth of Christ
(Über die Geburt Jesu)

Night more than bright, night brighter than the day,
brighter than sun, night when light came about,
that light which God, light housed in light, chose out.
Did ever day or night such light display!
Oh joyful night, in which were made away
despair and dark and all the devil's plot,
when horror and hell-fear were put to rout.
Sky splits, but now the thunder stands at stay.

He who made nights and times tonight comes down
to bow to time and put our body on,
making us over his eternal right.
The cloudy night of grief, sin's blinded black,
the very dark of death must now fall back
before this day-bright, brighter-than-bright night.

On his birthday
(Auf seinen Geburtstag)

That thou art maker of this fair world's frame
and the vast host of starbright endlessness
wherein the several planets keep their place
according to thy laws, and in thy name,
that thou with such adornment hast graced them,
and most, our own, with faces numberless,
unlike, yet like, which are thy witnesses
that thou alone art nothing like nor same,
all this I praise, yet more, that thou hast made
me apt to praise thy wonders, and hast shed
light in my opened eyes, I praise all this,
yet more, that thou wilt show me what the room
of earth holds not; wilt promise me thy home,
and more, thyself, for whom there is no praise.

Friedrich von Logau 1604-1655

Born into the aristocracy of Silesia, on his family estate of Brockut. After a childhood and schooling constantly interrupted by war, he studied law at Altdorf and in 1633 entered into possession of his estate, which was heavily encumbered with debts. To make matters worse, General Wallenstein's troops swept through the same year, and devastated the property. This finished any chance von Logau had of ever living on its income, and he became a public official in the service of his feudal overlords the dukes of Brieg, rising to high office.

He wrote almost nothing but epigrams, some three thousand of them, satirising all the traditional targets that go back to the Greek Anthology – women, fashion, doctors, changing times – on the basis that the old jokes are the best; and adding a few targets of his own as well. Despite his aristocratic background, he tended, because of his financial troubles and experience of war, to side with victims, especially the victims of war – peasant farmers, refugees, discharged soldiers. Like all good epigrammatists he is hard to translate at his best, both because his utterance is so condensed and because he often uses word-play which will not translate well. For over 100 years after his death, he was a forgotten poet in his own country, until the 18th-century writer Lessing reprinted his poems.

Might becomes Right
(Gewalt für Recht)

Through use and time, custom becomes the law;
for thirty years, our custom has been war.

Discharged Soldiers
(Abgedankte Soldaten)

Conscience sorely itching,
clothes in need of stitching,
bodies badly torn,
women too well-worn,
children (none of yours),
neither ox nor horse,
no pence in your wallets,
no food in your gullets,
that's what you who come
from the wars bring home.
Other pockets got
all the bloody loot.

The dead refugee
(Der Vertriebene redet nach seinem Tode)

What all my life I sought and could not find,
Death gives me now exactly to my mind.
I mean a house where no more death may come,
nor war, nor hunger hunt me from my home.

Merry Death
(Fröhlicher Tod)

Surely a man's death is a merry thing.
His heirs look forward to his burying,
the priests enjoy the alms of the poor sinner,
the worms delight in such a tasty dinner,
angels rejoicing trust they shall him save,
and Satan grins, in hopes his soul to have.

War and Peace
(Krieg und Friede)

We've fought for twenty years, but now at last
we shall have peace again, as in the past.
It's good to know what we were fighting for,
— just what we had before we went to war...

Paul Fleming 1609-1640

Born at Hartenstein in the Erzgebirge, near Leipzig, son of a Lutheran pastor. He studied medicine, rhetoric, dialectic and poetics at Leipzig and moved in a circle of poets, musicians and academics – a relatively peaceful life against a background of constant danger from war and plague. Its course altered when he joined a diplomatic-cum-trade mission sent by the duke of Holstein to the Persian court at Isfahan. The embassy had a journey like something out of Sinbad the Sailor, full of shipwrecks, brushes with Cossacks and other events which scarcely reflect in his poetry at all. The most important incident, from his point of view, was a stay the mission made at Tallinn in Estonia, where he met a German family called Niehusen. He fell in love with their daughter Elsabe and, by the time the embassy left, considered himself engaged. On his travels, however, he heard the news of her marriage. Possibly the 17th-century consciousness of transience in all human affairs made this easier to take; at all events he philosophically wrote her a congratulatory poem and, when the mission passed through Tallinn again on its way home, got engaged to her younger sister Anna. However, transience had not yet finished playing tricks on him. Before his marriage could take place, he died of pneumonia in Hamburg, aged 31.

In verse, Fleming was a technician, who loved playing with words and ideas. His love-poems especially are very much in the Petrarchist tradition; acrostic triumphs of wit and word-play. (In one poem to Anna, he momentarily forgot himself and used, word for word, a couplet from an earlier poem to her sister.) He is saved from aridity by his sense of humour, and by the genuine feeling in his poems on transience – when reading 'On a Corpse', one should remember that Fleming, as a medical student, had probably seen plenty.

Meditation
(Andacht)

I live, and yet not I. My life is he
who by his death begot the life in me.
My life was his death; in his death I live,
what he gave me, again to him I give,
he lives through my death. To myself I die
each day. My flesh, whose life is but a lie,
is my soul's grave. A timeless life to gain,
I in this finite world must rot and wane
while there is time. The soul's death comes too late
when his grim friend has snatched us from this state,
who feeds on flesh. Grant my soul grace, my Lord,
let not this body's custom harm thy ward.
My life, my death, my all, my nothing lies
within thee. If thou help, no danger is.
I help myself? I neither can nor may.
I leave it thee; the deeds are in thy sway,
I can but wish. I leave myself to thee.
I wish not to be mine. Give me thyself; take me.

Epitaph of a baited bear-cub
(Grabschrift eines jungen Bären, der gehetzet worden war)

I, who was young and little when I came,
dragged by the sturdy peasants, from my dam,
was bartered in the town and forced to ply
in freedom's stead the trades of slavery.

I, who was wild, grew tame; learned many a skill.
Yet has the world rewarded me but ill.
What was my sin, except the plump young fowl
that in my boldness many a time I stole?

Of all my life an endless dance was made,
and at the last I martyred am and dead.
Oh brothers mine and sisters, do not so.
Stay free, and never from your wild ways go.

On a corpse
(Bei einer Leichen)

Flashing light across the sky,
thin mist when the winds whirl round,
showers that scarcely wet the ground,
pistol shot, the smoke drifts by,
storms that threaten; quickly die,
empty valley echo-sound,
arrows when the mark is found,
soft ice when the sun is high.

These are things we well may call
empty and ephemeral,
but, as swiftly as they pass,
so your life, oh man, flies hence,
prisoner of transience.
All is nothing: you − its glass.

I am the Resurrection

(Ich bin die Auferstehung)

But I: all death and all defeat am I.
I cannot rise: I have not so much power,
but my acts need no help to bring me lower,
and how will pity find me where I lie?
Oh, that some saviour would but happen by!
Whom shall I lean on — in my saddest hour,
who's going to care? My fears and torments tower
above my fainting spirits to the sky.

And so I suffer, coward that I am,
and so I die, and no-one thinks it shame,
yet to die to myself is what I need.
Come life, come resurrection speedily!
I am in sin a dead man; rescue me,
or I shall be for ever down and dead.

Christian Hofmann von Hofmannswaldau
1617-1679

Born in Breslau, Silesia, a year before the outbreak of the
Thirty Years' War. This, the main event of his times, the
main theme of most of his contemporaries' work, plays
almost no overt role in his poems. There are some practical
reasons for this. His family was aristocratic and rich; wealth
and travel could protect him to some extent from the war's
effects. But its absence from his work is the result of
conscious decision. He loved life, and all the pleasure he
could (without harming anyone else) get out of it. He had a
keen appreciation of all forms of sensual pleasure and says
in one poem that those who have no such appreciation, or
consider it wrong, are 'stepsons of nature' who have 'lost
their taste for the world'. The only time the world tasted
sour to Hofmannswaldau was when he thought of losing it,
and his reaction to whatever threatened the pleasure he
enjoyed was to turn away. (It should not, however, be
assumed from his poems that he was a libertine in anything
but theory; he had a long and happy marriage and no
recorded mistresses. Of course he might just have been
good at covering his tracks.)

His delight in language and metre is as sensual as his
delight in women. His language and imagery look ornate
beside those of his good friend Gryphius (an attraction of
opposites, one presumes), and in a relatively small body of
work he uses sixty-six different stanza forms, many
intended to go to music. The only lack of variety is in the
theme; give or take a few humorous epitaphs and remarks
on Italian literature, love and the sensual pleasure which
accompanies it account for his entire work.

Poem in praise of the most amiable of womankind

(Lob-rede an das lieb-wertheste frauen-zimmer)

Most precious ladies, sunshine in our mind,
choice jewels who adorn our streets and houses,
what man of stone is hostile to your kind,
you conquerors of everything in trousers?
When all your beauty's wares are on display
who'd stand before you; who so bold and mighty?
To such divinities who would not pray,
the living likenesses of Aphrodite?
However, I shall only touch upon
two of your charms; my senses' ship has landed
on those soft shores where waves of milk are blown
by none but love's light breeze.... To be quite candid,
it's breasts I have in mind; those marble hills
where love's pavilion rises up and topples
at a mere breath; on which the sun's gold spills
its perfumed light. They are those Eden-apples
which every Adam longs to nibble at,
a pleasure-park, two cliffs caressed by zephyrs,
a crystal spring whose streams are honey-sweet,
a pure white altar where the whole world offers.
Two sisters sleeping chastely on one pillow,
two armouries for Cupid's ammunition,
a kindling that can warm the coldest fellow,
a lime that holds the senses in submission.
Unheard-of wealth, cordial to cure the dead,
rubies in alabaster, honeycomb
where weary souls lick sweetness, the good bread
of heaven, love's stars lighting the wide room
of space. They are a sword, hacking deep wounds,
a winter-blooming rose-bush; they're an ocean
on which poor sailors hear the siren sounds,
two snowy Aetnas lit by sparks of passion

that melt hard steel. A pond of silver fish
to sate love's appetite, all pleasure's tinder,
a wreath where virtue blooms, youth's only wish,
a blaze of snow, a pastime and a wonder.
They're love's round coffin, key to every heart,
the seat of joy, flowing with milk and nectar,
two decoy-birds, that trap free men for sport,
two brilliant suns that blind the rash inspector
even through mist.... They are a dress of silk
so thin, that you can see each threadlike vein,
two chalky hills, two churns of fancy's milk,
two purest wells that never want for rain.
Two hunters, who trap in and out of season,
two snowballs women aim at poor men's peace,
two snares, too subtle for the sharpest reason,
two stalls on which the wares of love and grace
are on display; wares that no merchant can
acquire, except his lips would be the banker,
two market-baskets full of marzipan
after whose sweetness thirsty mouths will hanker.
Two noble towers of ivory where Cupid
stands sentry with his bow, two gems that gleam
on women's bodies as they fool men stupid,
a bellows fanning an eternal flame.
Ruby and pearl, met in a marriage-bower
where almond's milk washes the rose, its neighbour,
a sea-compass that bids the weary rower
pull like the devil to gain pleasure's harbour.
Love's throne, glazed lily-white, a sacred shrine
where hearts kneel humbly down and chaste lips kiss,
a sea of joy and sensuousness, a mine
of diamonds.... Tell me, why should you screen this?
Why cover such a useful pair of globes
and hide the latitude of love's own country?
Oh beautiful; believe me, all your robes
can't cheat the keen glance of a loving sentry.

The lighthouse of your breast gleams through the mist
of silk you wear, guiding some lucky sailor
into love's harbour where he takes his rest
while I'm still storm-tossed, busy with the baler.
It's well for him who lives so at his ease,
who hides from grief, with that white shield for warden,
who feeds on milk and honey all his days,
who sits at leisure in the lily-garden,
who gathers flowers in a snowy meadow,
who mines the rubies from the richest lode,
who plucks the roses out of the thorns' shadow,
who has the sweet strong apples for his food,
whom fortune loves so well, it calls him brother,
who loves the breast he makes his pillow of,
who flies, unhesitating, to his lover
and floods her with the liquid balm of love.

Epitaph of an incompetent doctor
(Grabschrift eines unwissenden Arztes)

Death's trusty sergeant lies beneath this stone,
whose fell prescriptions struck so many down.
I wonder that death took him; it seems hard,
so true a servant, and so small reward.

Transient Beauty
(Vergänglichkeit der Schönheit)

Chaste as you are, yet sallow Death one day
shall let his chill hand wander on your breast.
Your lips' bright brittle coral soon shall waste;
your warm snow shoulders dwindle to cold clay.
Your eyes' sweet flash he'll douse, your hand he'll stay;
before his might such frailties stand not fast.
Your hair, whose light left gold behind, at last
like an old ribbon time shall sweep away.

Your shapely foot, your movements' loveliness,
if they come not to dust, shall come to less.
Your beauty's worshippers you then shall want.
These, and much more than these, in time must fade;
only your heart can last till time is dead,
since nature made it hard as adamant.

Epitaph of Mary Magdalen
(Grabschrift Mariae Magdalenae)

Here rests the lovely head; here the light lap
whence flowed enticement like a melting sap.
Since this sweet woman left the trade of whore,
angels themselves come courting at her door.

Of the time when Flavia was with him in the country
(Als Flavia sich neben ihm einst auf dem Lande befand)

Turning my clouded eyes toward that place
where Flavia sat by me some time ago,
– I plucking from the white field of her face
lilies and roses that in soft clefts grow –
I sigh: fair wood, your beauties now you lack,
but Flavia is not lacking; seek her here.
The day that bore me I would call most black,
but that her image in my thoughts shines clear.
Forest: your green surrenders to the snow,
her likeness in my mind lives constantly,
and if pale death caressed me now, I know
my heart would take her to my grave with me.

Epitaph of an alchemist
(Grabschrift eines Alchimisten)

On a new art I bent my learned mind:
the secret that from death would set me free.
That which I sought so long, I did not find,
and what I never sought came to find me.

Catharina Regina von Greiffenberg 1633-1694

An Austrian-born gentlewoman, who spent most of her life in Nuremberg. Much of the power and energy of 17th-century German verse came from Silesia in the north, partly because Martin Opitz, the first man since mediaeval times to instigate a real revival in German poetry, was a Silesian. The poetry of the south was more ornate, more fanciful, more Catholic (though Catharina, as it happens, was a Lutheran), and it centred on Nuremberg and the literary society of the *Pegnesischer Blumenorden,* of which Catharina was a member, together with her friend the poet Sigmund von Birken. Her poems were first published by Birken, together with Rudolf von Greiffenberg, who was successively Catharina's uncle, guardian and husband.

Her only theme is religion, which for her is a powerful intoxicant. This is where the south seems a stronger influence on her than Lutheranism; although she shares the *beliefs* of her fellow-Lutherans Gryphius and Fleming, their sober, meditative *attitude* is alien to her; she tends rather to ecstasy. Her two favourite images, recurring throughout her work, are blood and fire. Her bold and experimental use of language, particularly in coining compound words, is not unique for the time. Schottelius in his *Teutsche Sprachkunst* of 1641 had stressed the peculiar facility of German for word-compounding. But it is doubtful if anyone ever took it further – her more extreme examples can be dazzling, and quite untranslatable.

Of the inexpressible inspiration of the Holy Spirit

(Über das unaussprechliche Heilige Geistes-Eingeben)

Lightning invisible, darkbrightening light,
passionfilled power, most elusive being,
within my soul something of God has being,
that steers and stirs me: I sense a strange light.
No soul is of itself so lauded-light;
a wonderwind, a spirit, a weaving being,
the timeless breathforce, self-essence of being,
kindled in me the heavenleaping light.

Rainbowglassimage, wonderbright you shine,
still shimmering, unfathomably clear,
the doveflight of the soul in suntruthshine.
The moon's god-troubled surface too is clear;
it faces full into the spiritshine
at first; then turns; looks down, earthward and clear.

Of my Christ's bloody expense of love and pain

(Über meines Jesu blutigen Lieb- und Schmerzen-Schweiss)

My sap of saving, my elected blood,
how praise, how prize the high heart-tearing test
of constancy; how may it be expressed
if heaven lend me not the praising mood?
Salvation's lymph and pulse, convulsing flood
of lovepain from a torture-molten breast,
God's Son sinks down under your climbing crest.
His heart lives less in him than does our good,

for one is spilt, the other gained thereby.
Each drop's a glass, wherein his grace is shown.
Through bloodpain glitters godly majesty;
bearing all guilt, yet was he not borne down.
Blood: save my parting soul, for if I wear
your crimson robe, I need no judgment fear.

Simon Dach 1605-1659

Born in Memel, Silesia, he associated with a circle of poets centred at Königsberg, who followed the poetic theories of the Silesian poet and critic Martin Opitz. This profoundly influential man not only instigated the 17th-century revival in German poetry but laid down 'rules' for its diction, imagery and metre which were widely accepted. He didn't, for instance, approve of dactyls, so for a long time they were simply not used, until the southern poets led by Klaj at Nuremberg began experimenting with them. Dach was very much Opitz's follower, particularly in the sobriety of his diction and imagery and the rational piety of his tone. The Königsberg poets wrote mainly on religious themes and events within their own circle – births, marriages and deaths among their friends and patrons. The poem here translated was addressed to one Councillor Andreas Holländer on the death of his son, and is typical of Dach's quiet, low-key approach. He seems to have been a gentle, amiable man whose life, like his work, centred on his family and friends. Like Gryphius and Logau, he had to contend with bad health all his life.

Poem of condolence
(Trostgedicht)

If, son, your innocence has taken wing
high above air, in heaven again to see
grandpa and grandma: angel if you be,
deep in the flowers of a timeless spring,
if, sharp of answer, quick in questioning,
unstudied lore you fathom and lay free,
however lost you are in ecstasy,
look down and see your kinsfolk suffering.

Your father lays you bitterly to rest,
your mother's grief tears at her hair and breast,
your sisters' cheeks are pale; they weep their blood.
If you see this, condemn these anguished cries,
give them yourself wise counsel, kind advice,
for human comfort seems to do no good.

Johann George Albinus 1624-1679

I know next to nothing about Albinus, except that in 1675, when he published the book from which this poem comes, he was a pastor in Weissenfels, near Leipzig. His book, *Geistlich-geharnischter Kriegesheld* ('The spiritually-armoured war hero') was a collection of soldiers' songs, treating both actual warfare and the daily hardships of camp and march. They were set to popular hymn tunes, so that soldiers could actually sing them. From his familiarity with details of army life, and his identification with the soldiers of his songs, I should guess that Albinus had really been a soldier, or army chaplain, but I could well be wrong – it must have been quite easy, in those days, to gain a closer acquaintance with military matters than one wanted.

Song to be sung when besieging a town
(Belägerungs-Lied)

Unless the Lord God be allied
with us throughout this siege;
unless His grace strike on our side
and turn from us the edge
of hostile steel, then we shall have
no choice but shamefully to leave
what we so much desire.

Though in the town the enemy
has sheltered all his power,
and planted great artillery
on top of every tower,
let that town fall, Lord, to our share,
with everything that lives in there,
give it us, Lord, for loot!

To judge by all the cannon-sound,
the enemy's still able.
Each breakfast-time, he sends around
some firebombs for our table.
Spiked cudgels, sabres, battle-steel,
all these and more, with right goodwill,
he would present to us.

Nor will our foe become our friend
the day we storm the walls;
they'll stay the same, right to the end,
our enemies in their souls.
They'll make a sortie, furious,
and use grenades to murder us
in full view of the town.

So, Lord, turn all their pride to shame,
deliver us their town,
and let their wealth, too much for them,
now profit us alone.
Chastise their arrogance and state
by taking that which made them great,
since they won't give it up.

Give them all; woman, man and child,
into our hands, O Lord;
let fire's terror drive them wild,
that they lay down the sword.
Let our attack be not in vain,
Lord; give us but this town, and then
we'll sing Thy praise. Amen.

Theodor Storm 1817-1888

Born in the sea-town of Husum, up near the Danish border. He is now remembered more for his prose than his verse, particularly the novella *Der Schimmelreiter (Rider on a White Horse).* He was perhaps the greatest exponent of that style of writing known as Biedermeier, which was a conscious reaction against the excesses of Romanticism. The differences might be briefly summed up thus: the Romantics were terminally self-obsessed, affected a sentimental worship of 'nature', a subject of which they knew almost nothing, and admired great men, by which they generally meant men who killed a spectacular number of people, Napoleon being the prime example. The Biedermeier group looked for their themes rather to the world outside than to themselves; their attitude to the natural world was one of informed respect, and their heroes are men who achieved some practical good for their community, preferably without getting famous – the hero of *Der Schimmelreiter* is a man whose life-work is the improvement of the local dyke, no minor matter in Schleswig-Holstein. Storm's landscape poems are resolutely unsentimental and matter-of-fact – no Romantic would ever have looked closely enough at a beetle to notice that its casing resembled armour.

Aside
(Abseits)

It's very quiet; the heath's asleep
in the warm radiance of noon.
A sort of pinkish haze takes shape
around the graveyard's mellow stone.
The blooms are open; their scents rise
into the blue of summer skies.

Beetles in golden coats of mail
traverse the gorse, busy and quick,
and on each separate heatherbell
the clustered bees are hanging thick.
In the dense growth, there is a stir
of birds, and larksong fills the air.

A cottage, shabby, tumbledown,
stands bathed in sun and loneliness.
At his half-door, a working man
contentedly observes the bees.
Perched on a stone nearby, his lad
is cutting whistles out of reed.

A far clock makes the air, so still,
vibrate with one faint stroke of time.
The old man lets his eyelids fall
and harvests honey in his dream.
No other sound of our mad days
can pierce this lonely, aside place.

Baltic Shore
(Meeresstrand)

Dark's drawing close; the gull
is off to the lagoon,
and on the mudflat mirror
the late light glances down.

From somewhere near the water
grey fowl scurry past.
The sea-islands are hanging
like dreams in the mist.

I hear the whispered secrets
of the unquiet ooze,
and the sad solo birdcalls.
That's how it always was.

The wind gives a slight shiver
and falls still. You can hear
the voices over the water;
they've become quite clear.

Newspaper advertisement in August
(August: Inserat)

I courteously request the dear young sirs
who are proposing to purloin my pears
this season, and my apples, to confine
themselves, as far as may be, to this line
of harmless fun, and to eschew the sport
of trampling down my peas as they depart.

To Klaus Groth
(An Klaus Groth)

When dark comes on,
and life, and thee, both quieten down;
when tha just lets thy tired hand fall
down on thy knee, and from the wall
tha hears the clock, whose voice were drowned
before, in all the daytime sound;
when every corner's heaped wi' shade
and all night's creatures wake outside,
when then once more thy window-pane
catches the sun, and gold floods in,
and, afore sleep comes wi' the night,
just one more time, life flares up bright,
that's summat to warm any man,
when dark comes on.

(This poem was written in the Holstein dialect, in tribute to the poet
to whom it is addressed, Storm's fellow-Holsteiner. Groth used
dialect for his own poems. At the time of this poem, both men were
elderly.)

Thoughts about cats
(Von Katzen)

On May-day last, my cat gave birth to six
endearing little kittens, pussywillows,
all white with small black tails... it really was
the sweetest of maternities! My cook,
however, (cooks are all a callous lot;
a kitchen's no place for humanity),
she wanted to have five of the six drowned.
Five pussywillows with black tiny tails
this blasted female wished to do to death.
I soon gave her what for! Humanity,
I thought, earns blessings. Well, the little pets
grew up, and soon were trotting with their tails
stiff in the air, all over hearth and home.
(The cook looked on and plotted felicide.)
They grew, and every night beneath her window
they tried out their delightful little voices.
I praised myself and my humanity,
watching them grow.... A twelvemonth has gone by,
my kits are cats, and May-day's here again,
and how shall I describe the awesome scene?
Throughout my house, from cellar up to attic,
each corner seems to be a labour ward.
They're lying under staircases and tables,
in cupboards, baskets... the old matriarch
– oh no, it's too unspeakable – is lying
in what was once the cook's virginal bed,
and each cat in the house, every last one,
has seven, think about it, seven kittens,
all pussywillows, white with small black tails.
The cook is raving, and I don't know how
I'm to set bounds to this virago's rage.

She wants to murder the whole forty-nine,
and as for me, I'm going round the bend.
Alas, humanity! Oh, what the devil
am I to do with six-and-fifty cats?

Stefan George 1868-1933

Born at Büdesheim, in the Rhineland, brought up bilingual in French and German, he wrote in both, plus English, Dutch, Italian and a language of his own invention. A loner who attracted numerous literary 'disciples' (their term); an elitist, one of whose books, written for a small circle of friends, became a huge popular hit with First World War soldiers; a man whose lifestyle could be insufferably pretentious, yet whose best poems are painfully clear-sighted and honest. He dreamed of a 'new kingdom' (das neue Reich) of culture and beauty, not to be confused with the third Reich – he undoubtedly despised democracy, but his idea of a ruling elite was a conclave of cultivated persons, not a bunch of brainsick thugs. Goebbels offered him honours, which he made a point of declining through his Jewish disciple Ernst Morwitz, and he died in exile in Switzerland soon after.

His faithful disciples boosted his reputation sky-high for some years; inevitably the pendulum then swung back until he was right out of fashion. For me he is the poet, above all others, who consistently couches his thought in words so right as to seem inevitable. Second best would never do for him; time and again one finds a phrase that simply could not be altered except for the worse.

The poem 'Trauer', here translated, was personal; the 'mourning' was for one Maximilian Kronberger, who died at sixteen of meningitis. For the previous two years, the then middle-aged George had been in love with him, or thought he was. His grief, at any rate, was comprehensive and long-lasting.

Mourning II
(Trauer II)

The forest ails
aloud; adorned for nothing with new green.
The field you should have hallowed freezes now;
it's waiting for the sun, and you've gone in.
Frail grassblades shiver on the slopes of hills
where now you never go. ·

The buds that you don't wake will go to waste;
likewise the twigs you don't plait any more.
If *you* don't pick them, what are flowers for;
what good is fruit that you can never taste?

Trees crashing to the earth
in the young copse; when will they cut
the next? The morning green looks tired;
grass lies in swathes, and it had scarce appeared.
No birdsong; only the wind's frosty mirth,
then axes ringing out.

Southern coast: bay
(Südlicher Strand: Bucht)

I have been working up and down this coast,
this glittering string of towns, a weary while,
preparing here and there a wedding-feast....
A stranger walks out of the hall.

I grow no wiser for the time I linger
on these same bridges; I just hurt the more.
I still let old hopes twist me round their finger,
I still go haunting many a door,

and when up there the dancing has begun
for the bright couples in their finery,
I follow the poor tramps down to the quay...
it hurts so much to walk alone.

Was ist geschehn dass ich mich kaum noch kenne

What's happened, that I hardly know myself?
I'm no-one else, yet more than once I was.
Those who have loved and honoured me still do;
companions, shy and pleasing, seek me out,
and nothing I once had is lost to me,
not summer joys, proud dreams, nor gentle kisses....
My very blood beats bolder. I was poor
as long as I took care, but since I gave
myself away, I have myself complete.

The word
(Das Wort)

From dream or distance, I would bring
to my land's border some strange thing,

then wait until the grey Norn came,
and from her well fished out its name.

Then I could take good hold of it,
and now, all round, it flowers bright.

Once, from a voyage blessed with luck,
I brought a fragile gemstone back.

She looked and looked and said: 'It's clear
there's no name waiting for that here',

whereon it slipped out of my hand,
and never came to grace my land.

I learned the rules through suffering:
where no word is, can be no thing.

Noch zwingt mich treue über dir zu wachen

Faith makes me still watch over you; the beauty
of your long-suffering makes me remain.
I cultivate grief like a sacred duty,
that I may the more truly share your pain.

No warm appeal will ever give me greeting;
as long as we're together, I must know,
submissive and afraid, the hurt that's waiting
for those who find their fortunes in the snow.

Nicht ist weise bis zur letzten frist

Foolish are the tenants of the past
who hang on till the lease expires at last.
Southwards, seawards, birds are flying now;
flowers wither, waiting on the snow.

They're so tired, you twine them timidly.
This year, they're the last that we shall see.
Don't ask more; they cannot come to you.
Wait; perhaps one spring we'll see them new.

Let my arm go now, and steel your mind,
and we'll leave the last late sun behind.
Mists across the mountain creeping come.
Leave now, before winter hunts us home!

Komm in den totgesagten park und schau

Come in the park they say is dead, and see
the shimmering smile of shores in distant haze,
the blue beyond hope, the clouds' clarity
distilling light on waters and bright ways.

Break there the deep gold and the gentle grey
of birch and box: softly the breezes play.
Late roses linger, still some way from death.
Choose them and kiss them; make of them a wreath.

Don't forget these late asters, nor the vine
left to run wild, its tendrils crimson-wound,
and all the green life that may yet be found
into the mood of autumn mildly twine.

Sources for translations

Christine de Pisan –
Christine de Pisan: ballades, rondeaux and virelais, ed.
K. Varty (Leicester University Press, 1963).

Charles d'Orléans –
Charles d'Orléans: Poésie, ed. P. Champion, (CFMA, Paris,
1923-27).

Walther von der Vogelweide –
Walther von der Vogelweide: Gedichte, ed. P. Wapnewski
(Fischer Bucherei, Frankfurt a.M., 1966).

Heinrich von Morungen, Hartmann von Aue –
Minnesang vom Kürenberger bis Wolfram, ed. M. Wehrli
(Francke Verlag Bern, no date).

Andreas Gryphius –
Andreas Gryphius: Gedichte, ed. A. Elschenbroich (Reclam,
Stuttgart, 1968).

Friedrich von Logau –
Friedrich von Logau: Sinngedichte, ed. E.P. Wieckenberg
(Reclam, Stuttgart, 1984).

Paul Fleming –
Paul Fleming: Gedichte, ed. J. Pfeifer (Reclam, Stuttgart,
1964).

Christian Hofmann von Hofmannswaldau –
Christian Hofmann von Hofmannswaldau: Gedichte, ed. M.
Windfuhr (Reclam, Stuttgart, 1969).

Catharina Regina von Geiffenberg –
Geistliche Sonnette, Lieder und Gedichte, collected by Hans
Rudolf von Greiffenberg (Michael Enders, Bayreuth, 1662).

Simon Dach –
Simon Dach: Gedichte, ed. W. Ziesemer (Niemayer, Halle,
1937).

Johann George Albinus, Georg Rudolf Weckherlin –
Epochen der deutschen Lyrik 1600-1700, ed. C. Wagen-
knecht (dtv Munchen, 1982).

Theodor Storm –
Theodor Storm: Werke, ed. H. Engelhardt (Cotta, Stuttgart, 1958).

Stefan George –
Stefan George: Werke, ed. H. Kupper vormals Bondi (Dusseldorf u., Munchen, reissued 1968).

Acknowledgements

Certain of the translations of Gryphius, von Logau, Fleming and von Hofmannswaldau have appeared in issues 3 and 4 of *Babel*.